GOD MAKES
MY LITTLE TAIL
Wiggle

THE BOOK OF PRAYERS

BOB & CODY WOLFF

GOD MAKES
MY LITTLE TAIL
Wiggle

THE BOOK OF PRAYERS

BOB & CODY WOLFF

Published by
Tail Wiggle, LLC
10400 Overland Road, Suite 143
Boise, Idaho, USA 83709

Book Information:
www.CodyandBob.com
Cody & Bob ™
Tail Wiggle ™
Facebook: /codyandbobinspires
Instagram: @codyandbob

Library of Congress: 9781949653229

Hardcover Print ISBN: 978-1-949653-92-2
Paperback Print ISBN: 978-1-949653-80-9
eBook ISBN: 978-1-949653-18-2
Audio Book ISBN: 978-1-949653-11-3

Inspirations

1

2

A BEST FRIEND CALLED YOUR PAST 31

3

THE GIFT OF PEOPLE IN YOUR LIFE 41

4

LOVING YOURSELF AND THE GIFT CALLED YOUR LIFE   55

5

YOU'VE BEEN CREATED FOR A GREAT PURPOSE   61

6

THE POWER OF FAITH TO CHANGE YOUR LIFE   65

7

LISTENING TO THE VOICE WITHIN   **79**

8

FOLLOWING THE INSPIRATION WITHIN   **87**

9

GOING FROM WHERE YOU ARE TO ANYWHERE YOU WANT TO BE

97

10

YOU ARE AMAZING AND YOUR LIFE IS ABOUT TO BECOME EXTRAORDINARY

111

1

A FRESH WAY
OF THINKING FOR A NEW
WAY OF LIVING

> ## *I came into this life being happy, so what happened along the way?"*

Dear God,

You created me to be happy and to love this life. I'm so grateful for every moment and every day of it. Thank you. Help me to get back to being who I truly am. I let go of anything that keeps me from being the happy, joyful, playful, loving-my-life child of yours that I am. Thank you for speaking to me, in the ways I know it comes from you, to do your will, to dream my dreams, and to let your divine perfect guidance fill me with peace, power, presence and direction to every dream that is in divine perfect harmony with your plan for my life. I love you God. Thank you. Yes... Amen.

♥

Only happy thoughts come from God"

Dear God,

Thank you for being so good to me and blessing me. I let go of the endless chatter and conversations I have with myself and of thinking about anything and anyone whom I have let upset me about anything. I give you my thoughts and thank you for making them about the things that make me happy and will prosper and bless me and everyone I meet. Thank you. Yes... Amen.

♥

GOD MAKES MY LITTLE TAIL WIGGLE
www.CodyandBob.com

> **"Why is it that one of the hardest things to do is be easy on yourself?"**

Dear God,

Thank you for being so good to me. I'm so grateful that you love me with your divine perfect love even when I don't give myself that same love. It amazes me that after all these years, I'll sometimes have these feelings of unworthiness, guilt, and regret and that I should not or cannot receive your love, or another's love, or even my own love, because I don't deserve it. It's time to let all of that go. It's time for me to bless my past and all those in it and let it all go. Release it and them and let it all go to you so that I can open my heart and soul to let out the perfect divine child inside of me that is me. Let it all go so that I can fill my heart and overflow it with all the blessings to come into my life that you want to come into my life. Yes, dear God, the happy life I so want to live, love, and enjoy and share with others. Show me how to be my own best friend and to love that best friend with everything inside of me. Thank you. Yes... Amen.

♥

GOD MAKES MY LITTLE TAIL WIGGLE
www.CodyandBob.com

> *How would you feel, if you didn't think so much about how you felt?"*

Dear God,

For too long, I've been so demanding and tough on myself, and for what good reason? None! I'm shaking off the shackles of trying to please others. I'm letting go of trying to get others' approval. I'm saying goodbye to the endless critic inside of me who is never pleased and happy with anything I say or do and is always looking for things for me to feel bad about. None of that comes from you, God. It's all stuff that I've made up, and now I'm getting rid of it once and for all. The days and nights of feeling in a rut are over. I'm tired of looking down, and I'm now going to look up and out ahead in front of me at all the incredible things I can experience and enjoy. Thank you for showing me how to live my life filled with positive power, happy thoughts, joyful experiences, unlimited possibilities, and a head, heart, and soul overflowing with love. Thank you. Yes... Amen.

♥

GOD MAKES MY LITTLE TAIL WIGGLE
www.CodyandBob.com

> ## *You keep living with many beliefs that no longer benefit you"*

Dear God,

I so greatly appreciate your showing me the things I believe and how those things either bring me joy and happiness or take them away. Right now, I give you any beliefs that no longer serve me, and I let all of those go so I can start thinking about the things that will prosper and bless me from this moment on. Thank you. Yes... Amen.

♥

> *How much of your time each day is going towards something you want or pushing against something you don't?"*

Dear God,

Thank you for showing me how the past and those in it have been such amazing teachers. Everything that I have ever experienced always contains a blessing within it that has helped me to become who I am and has helped take me to where I am now. I know that life is a mirror and what I give out returns to me. I bless and send love to anyone and everyone in my life and let go of the past and only want the very best for anyone and everything that's ever been in it. I am so happy to begin this day fresh and brand new and for all the incredible opportunities and possibilities that are about to happen for me. Thank you. Yes... Amen.

♥

> *You can have what you want... just stop telling yourself and others what you have that's not what you want"*

Dear God,

Thank you for showing me the life-changing power in the things I think and the words I speak. Help me to speak of possibilities and not problems. Help me to speak positive words of faith and hope and encouragement to those who need it. Thank you for bringing those into my life who will inspire, uplift, and empower my life and for allowing me to do the same for them. Let my words be filled with unlimited divine inspirations that will lift me, and all those who hear them, to a life greater than we have ever known. Thank you. Yes... Amen.

♥

> ## *Talk more about how you want it and less about how it was"*

Dear God,

I bless everything and everyone in my past and let it and them go with blessings and love. Everything I've ever lived and anyone I've ever met have helped me to become who I am, and I'm so grateful for it all. I want to begin telling a new story, a happier story, an inspiring story of the person I desire to be and the life I desire to live. I know and believe my life can be as great as I allow it to be. I take the limits off of you and let go of any limitations, attitudes, and beliefs that have kept me where I am. Thank you for helping me to live the bigger, better, and most joyful life. You and I are the most powerful team, and together we can do amazing things that will touch people's lives for the best. Thank you. Yes... Amen.

♥

> # It's time to get over how you were raised, so that you can be raised higher"

Dear God,

Help me to know what living a bigger, better, and no-limits life can feel like. I let go of the limits I've placed upon myself. I ask that you fill my life with new blessings, abundance, greatness, and inspiration, plus the desire to do more, be more, experience more, enjoy more, and love more. Help me to believe bigger and live greater than I've ever known. With you, all things are possible. Thank you. Yes... Amen.

♥

GOD MAKES MY LITTLE TAIL WIGGLE
www.CodyandBob.com

"Compare? Don't you dare!"

Dear God,

Thank you for this great day and all the blessings you have given to me. Thank you for taking away the belief that the tougher I am on myself, the more you and others will love me. I know that is never true and will never be true. Your love is unconditional, and I want my love of me and for others to be the same too. You are amazing. I am amazing. We are all amazing. Thank you. Yes... Amen.

♥

GOD MAKES MY LITTLE TAIL WIGGLE
www.CodyandBob.com

> ## Other people's opinions will never be more important than your own"

Dear God,

I am thankful you are so loving, kind, and understanding with me. Oh, how I have spent too much time caring what others think about me and how it feels so empty and less than who I am each time I do. Thank you for showing that to me. Help me to trust myself more and more with each new day. Show me how to trust and rely on your perfect guidance and to listen to the voice inside of me that is your guidance and inspiration. Thank you. Yes… Amen.

♥

GOD MAKES MY LITTLE TAIL WIGGLE
www.CodyandBob.com

> **Worry yourself about none of it, because God is taking care of all of it"**

Dear God,

Thank you for showing me that you know nothing about worry and that I can be like you and not worry too. Help me to let go of anything that takes away my happiness and joy. Thank you for filling my life with only the things you want to bless me with, for they will only be those that will make me happy and are in divine perfect harmony with your plan and purpose for my life. Thank you. Yes... Amen.

♥

GOD MAKES MY LITTLE TAIL WIGGLE
www.CodyandBob.com

> *There's a big difference between what you'd like to experience and what you believe you can experience"*

Dear God,

Thank you for showing me how to dream a bigger dream. Thank you for calling and inspiring me to become higher, be better, be more, and live a life filled with love for you, me, this life, and everyone I meet. Help me to change my thinking from what I'd "like" to be, do, and have to what I "believe" I can be, do, and have. With you, dear God, all things are possible. With you, I can do all things because your strength, power, wisdom, well being, love, and blessings are always inside of me and surround me wherever I am and wherever I go. We are best friends and soulmates. I love you. Thank you. Yes... Amen.

♥

GOD MAKES MY LITTLE TAIL WIGGLE
www.CodyandBob.com

Just because you can't hear it or smell it doesn't mean it's not real"

Dear God,

Your power is simply amazing, and what's even more astounding is that I come from you. You created me! Thank you! Help me to increase my faith and belief in your unseen and unknown so that I may live a life of greatness, happiness, love, inspiration, and joy that I, and others, may know and be positively touched by. I feel your presence inside and all around me, God. I am yours. Thank you. Yes... Amen.

♥

GOD MAKES MY LITTLE TAIL WIGGLE
www.CodyandBob.com

> ## *I know nothing of..."*

Dear God,

You created me to be pure love, and that's what I am and will always be. As a child of yours, I'm made in your image. You created me for so many reasons, and nothing in this life is by randomness or chance. You are directing it all. I give you my life and everything in it so you can guide it to every blessing and every divinely inspired desire you give me that will always be for my divine perfect, highest, best good. Yes, I thank you for all my amazing blessings. I thank you for the gift of my life and for every moment of every day. I let go of any feelings and beliefs of unworthiness, and in their place I fill my life with love for me and for anyone and everyone else I meet. Thank you. Yes... Amen.

♥

> # *I live in a world of 'Yes' and 'Thank you'"*

Dear God,

I say "Yes" and Thank you" for every blessing in my life and all the new blessings and happy joyful experiences that are on the way to me. Help me to keep my thoughts and words on the things I want. I let go of the people and things that I've let hurt, anger, or upset me, or bring me unhappiness in any way, and wish them only love and blessings as I release them all. I fill my life with your divine perfect gifts and thoughts and, as I do, I feel my life getting better and better, every day and in every way. Thank you. Yes... Amen.

♥

"There is always a door that's open for you"

Dear God,

Thank you for the dreams and desires you give me. I know that you are my creator, protector, provider, and best friend and that you always have, and will always have, my divine best interests at the top of everything you do in my life. Starting today, I will have a new belief, faith, and trust in you to take me to every dream I have and to those I've yet to dream of, all in your divine perfect way and timing. You are amazing. I love you. Thank you. Yes… Amen.

♥

GOD MAKES MY LITTLE TAIL WIGGLE
www.CodyandBob.com

"Because I always believed it"

Dear God,

I am so grateful and thankful for the ability you have given to me to have faith, to trust, and to believe. For so long, I've believed in the life I've been living and that belief has kept creating the life I've been living. I'm ready to change that. I'm ready to trust again. Trust you, trust me, and trust us to make my life the amazing and blessed masterpiece you've created it and me to be. Take me to all the great and good you know I dream of and desire, and to the phenomenal I don't even know about yet but you do. Together, we are unstoppable. We are the best team. Let's touch the world with the gifts, talents, and abilities you've blessed me with. Let's make people's lives better in all the ways we can. I'm yours. I love you, dear God. Thank you. Yes... Amen.

♥

GOD MAKES MY LITTLE TAIL WIGGLE
www.CodyandBob.com

> ## *What you want is just a stretch away"*

Dear God,

Thank you for taking me out of the comfort zone and into the kind of thinking, ideas, faith, belief, and expectation that bring me to the greater life that's waiting for me outside that comfort zone. The place where your blessings and experiences are waiting for me to live, love, and enjoy. Help me to grow, be, do, and become all that you've created me to be. I take the limits off of you, dear God, and I'm ready for us to create the best life you have planned for me that can come only from you. Together we are unstoppable. Thank you. Yes... Amen.

♥

GOD MAKES MY LITTLE TAIL WIGGLE
www.CodyandBob.com

" *Never let your tail stop wiggling"*

Dear God,

I know that you've given me my life so that I can love and enjoy it. Thank you for it. I'm so grateful for all the things that make me happy and for all the things that are about to make me happy. I let go of thinking about anyone and anything that takes away my joy. In its place, I fill my life with happy thoughts, loving thoughts, empowering thoughts, and thoughts that fill me with your peace and presence. Thank you. Yes... Amen.

♥

GOD MAKES MY LITTLE TAIL WIGGLE
www.CodyandBob.com

2

A BEST
FRIEND CALLED
YOUR PAST

" *Then was so needed to get you to now* "

Dear God,

I am so thankful for everything that has happened to me because it's all helped me to become who I am and get me to where I stand right now. I bless all of the people and experiences that have been my teachers on this journey of life so far. I know that an amazing life of the right people and experiences is just waiting for me to discover. I'm so grateful that you're taking me to them and them to me in your divine perfect way. Thank you. Yes... Amen.

♥

> ## *Regret nothing. Bless everything."*

Dear God,

I'm so thankful for everything and everyone who has been in my past. I bless them, love them, and thank them and you for bringing all things and people who always work together for your and our divine perfect, highest, best good. Thank you for showing me how to move on and let go of my past so that I may live my life to the fullest and happiest today and all the days to come. I choose to spend my time thinking on the things and experiences I want and being so happy about today and tomorrow, for I know that's where I will be living the rest of my life. I'm so excited for all the things and blessings and experiences you have planned for me and for us to experience together. My life is incredible, and it's only going to get better. And it's all because of you. Thank you. Yes... Amen.

♥

GOD MAKES MY LITTLE TAIL WIGGLE
www.CodyandBob.com

"Everything is perfectly choreographed in your life"

Dear God,

Thank you for showing me the ways you are with me, guiding me, helping me and orchestrating everything in my life. I am so grateful for it all. I know and believe you created me for a special purpose—actually, many of them. I thank you for showing me all the reasons you created me and for helping me to become all that you know I can be. I let go of anything that keeps me from having and enjoying the best life and the blessings you have for me, and I trust your divine perfect plan for every part of my life. Thank you. Yes… Amen.

♥

> *Never be afraid to change anything in your life"*

Dear God,

I am so grateful for the desires you have placed inside of me. I know that the calling from you to a bigger, greater, and better life will never end, and I am so thankful for it. Thank you for helping me to let go of my fear of the unknown. Help me to replace my fears with faith and trust as you guide my life perfectly and divinely to anyone and everything for my divine perfect, highest, best good. Thank you. Yes... Amen.

♥

GOD MAKES MY LITTLE TAIL WIGGLE
www.CodyandBob.com

> "
> *Keep the past in your present if it brings you happiness and joy"*

Dear God,

Thank you for showing me how to make peace with my past and bless all those who have been a part of it. Each experience and each person gave me the perfect piece I needed at that time in my life to help me grow and move my thinking, believing, and life to the next step it needed to go and be. Help me keep my thoughts filled and overflowing with only the good, the positive, the inspiring, the encouraging, the hopeful, and the joyful. Thank you for showing me that a happy life is made up of happy thoughts and moments. Every day and in every way, my life keeps getting better and better. I'm so grateful for all of your help and blessings. I love you dear God. Thank you. Yes… Amen.

♥

GOD MAKES MY LITTLE TAIL WIGGLE
www.CodyandBob.com

> *Make the last experience of what you do a happy one, and you'll remember it for the rest of your life"*

Dear God,

Thank you for helping me be nicer, kinder, and better to myself. Thank you for helping me stop being so tough on myself and to stop beating myself up for not being this imaginary perfect person I've believed I should be. I know you see me as divinely created and just perfect as I am and will always be. I am so grateful for your showing me how to focus on the things that make me happy and all the new things you want me to experience, enjoy, and be blessed with. You are so good to me. Thank you. Yes... Amen.

♥

GOD MAKES MY LITTLE TAIL WIGGLE
www.CodyandBob.com

> *Keep looking forward, because that's where all the good stuff is"*

Dear God,

I so appreciate your showing me how the past was my teacher and how today and tomorrow are the places where I'm going to live and love the rest of my life. I bless and love anyone, everyone, and every experience I've ever had. Today is brand new, and so will be my every tomorrow. I want to live and enjoy them from where I now am and where you're going to take me to where I soon will be. I love you and am so grateful to you. Thank you. Yes... Amen.

♥

GOD MAKES MY LITTLE TAIL WIGGLE
www.CodyandBob.com

> ## "When looking back on your life, just remember... that was then, but this is Wow!"

Dear God,

I am so ready to live a new life of Wows. What happened back then will always be what happened back then and has nothing to do with me today, tomorrow, or any of the other days that will be waiting for me to live, love, enjoy, and discover. I thank you for being so understanding and loving with me. You know, better than I or anyone else, that I always want and try and do the very best I can at the time I'm doing it. And you always whisper to me, with the voice within that I know comes from you, that the best I can do and know at the time I think about and do it, will always be just perfect, because you wouldn't allow anything to happen in my life unless it is for my divine perfect and highest, best good, and according to your plan for me and my life. You know, dear God, the more I think about it, the more I realize something amazing: I've never made any mistakes! Everything and everyone that's ever been or will ever be a part of my life in any way, is there and will be there for a divine reason and because it all fits perfectly into your divinely amazing plan for this gift you've given me called My Life! I love you so much, God. Thank you with all of my heart and soul for everyone and everything. I bless and love it and them all! Thank you. Yes... Amen.

♥

GOD MAKES MY LITTLE TAIL WIGGLE
www.CodyandBob.com

3

THE GIFT
OF PEOPLE IN
YOUR LIFE

> *Family and friends see you as the way you were and not as the way you are and have become*"

Dear God,

I am so grateful and appreciate everything and everyone in my life. I release the old attitudes and beliefs about anyone and anything. Each day is a brand new day and with it, I'm created new. Thank you for helping me to grow in positive, loving, inspiring, and empowering ways. I let go of the old so that the new you want to bring me can come into my life. The past is behind me, and so are the attitudes and ideas that go along with it. I'm a blessed child of yours, and from this day on I will treat myself and all those in my life and those who will be, as the always-changing, always-growing, loving creations of yours that we are. Thank you. Yes… Amen.

♥

GOD MAKES MY LITTLE TAIL WIGGLE
www.CodyandBob.com

> **Those who've known you the longest aren't always those who know you the best"**

Dear God,

I am so blessed in so many ways. Thank you. I realize that everyone who is in my life is there for a reason and some will be in it only for a season. I let go of the expectation that someone else is supposed to make me happy or understand me. You make me happy, God. I make me happy by the thoughts I think, the dreams I have, and opening my heart and soul and mind to your guidance and direction. You created me. You know anything and everything about me, even all the things I've yet to discover. Help me and take me to all that I can be. Let my life be a blessing to all who know, see, and hear about me. I'm so grateful and thankful to you, dear God. I love you. Thank you. Yes... Amen.

♥

GOD MAKES MY LITTLE TAIL WIGGLE
www.CodyandBob.com

> **When you look to others to fill your happiness tank, don't be surprised to find the fuel gauge always reading low"**

Dear God,

Thank you for awakening something inside of me that is inspiring me to live my life the way I want and desire. You created me and I'm a child of yours, and you give me all the direction, help, protection, blessings, and everything I can want or need to live the life of my dreams wherever you and those dreams and desires call me to. I let go of the opinions of others and choose to live from my own opinion, because nobody knows me, or my life, better than you and I. Thank you. Yes... Amen.

♥

> "Here's an easy way to know who to spend time with: Does that person spend more time talking about problems or possibilities?"

Dear God,

Thank you for showing me that I do have a choice in the people and family I choose to spend time with. I let go of the guilt and the feeling of obligation to anyone I know is not right for my divine, highest, best good. I release them with love and blessings and wish only the very best for them always. I so appreciate your bringing the right people, the best people, into my life, and me into theirs, so that we all can grow, experience, enjoy, and love this life and each other, and know that everything is divinely ordered, just the way you want it to be. You are my best friend, God. I love you. Thank you. Yes... Amen.

♥

> *You live in a world where there are more people who'll tell you why you can't do something, than those who'll tell you why you can. Find those who'll tell you why you can."*

Dear God,

For so long I've made compromises and have accepted people and things in my life that I knew deep down were not bringing me happiness. I know now that I don't have to accept anything less than only the things I want and desire because I deserve them. Dear God, I have so much to give to others. I have so much to give to myself and to this world that I'm so grateful to you I'm blessed to live in. Let me think and believe in a bigger and greater way, one I know I'm worthy of. Help me to let go of anyone and anything that keeps me from living in the happiness you've created me to live, love, and enjoy. Thank you for bringing the best people and experiences into my life that are in perfect harmony with my purpose you've created me to know and to live. This is a new day. This is a fresh new beginning, and I'm so thankful to you for it all. I love you, God. Thank you. Yes... Amen.

♥

GOD MAKES MY LITTLE TAIL WIGGLE
www.CodyandBob.com

> *Choose carefully those you spend time with, for they will not let you rise any higher than what they are thinking, believing, or living without trying to make you feel guilty or an outcast"*

Dear God,

Thank you for bringing into my life the right people who will be my true friends and will know, understand, encourage, and inspire me to a greater, bigger, happier, and more joyful and fulfilling inspired life. Thank you for helping and showing me how to do the same for them. I bless all the family and friends who are and have been in my life, and I want only the very best for them. I release anyone and anything from my life that keeps me from doing your will. You created me for your purpose, and I want to live it and love it. You are with me always, and I am with you always. Together we are the best for each other. I love you, God. Thank you. Yes... Amen.

♥

> *Let go of who and what's not ready for you, so that those who are and that which is can come into your life"*

Dear God,

This is going to be the day when I let go. Let go of the old beliefs and the old ways of thinking and doing things. I bless them all, for I know they've all helped get me to the place where I am at this moment. I am so ready for a new beginning, a fresh new start and brand new chance to begin something new in my life. As I let the old past and its ways go, I open every door to you, dear God, to flood and overflow my life with your blessings, abundance, love, and experiences that I can feel deep inside of me that you're calling me to. Take this blessed life of mine that I'm so grateful and thankful for and make me, and it, into everything you know and want it to be. I'm ready and I'm yours, dear God. I love you with everything inside my heart and soul. Thank you. Yes... Amen.

♥

> **Spend more time with those who celebrate you and less time with those who tolerate you"**

Dear God,

I celebrate this moment when I'm thinking about you and how truly, incredibly blessed I am. Thank you! I love you and I love me. Thank you for bringing into my life the right people for the right reasons. Thank you for all of us being inspirations to each other. I'm so grateful to have people in my life who love, support, and encourage me, and I love doing the same for them. Friends are one of your greatest gifts that I can experience in this blessed life, and I thank you for every one of them. I ask that you bless all of us in every way, as we live our lives to the dreams you are calling us to. Let me be your hands and feet and let my actions and words help make your other children's lives better, happier, more joyful, and touched by our love. Thank you. Yes... Amen.

♥

GOD MAKES MY LITTLE TAIL WIGGLE
www.CodyandBob.com

> *Blessed be those who ask you about and remind you of the things that are your passions, dreams, and desires"*

Dear God,

One of the things I've learned in this life is that you created people for each other. We are meant to love and care for one another like we do for ourselves. So many times, I get so involved and self-absorbed in my own world that I don't give friends, family, and others the love and attention I know I could give if I really wanted to. Help me to change that, dear God. You created me for a purpose higher and greater than myself, and one in which I can help and inspire others; to give this world and the people in it my gifts and talents that you have so lovingly blessed me with so I can help make their lives better in some way. Show me all the gifts and talents you've blessed me with, and teach me how to use them to fullest of my God-given abilities. Open every door for me so that I can take who and what you've created me to be, to make this world, its people, and my life, the best they can be. Thank you so much, dear God. I love you. Thank you. Yes... Amen.

♥

GOD MAKES MY LITTLE TAIL WIGGLE
www.CodyandBob.com

> ## "Blessings shared are blessings doubled"

Dear God,

I let go of thinking I need to know it all, do it all, keep it all, and not share the things in my life with those I love and with those who love me. Thank you for bringing into my life the right people, animals, and anything else at the right time for the right reasons. Thank you for inspiring me to share my life with those you've put into my life at this moment for your divine perfect reasons, and for inspiring them to share theirs with me. Help me to inspire and love them and let them love and inspire me as we all lift each other to lives of higher and greater joy, purpose, and love. Thank you. Yes... Amen.

♥

GOD MAKES MY LITTLE TAIL WIGGLE
www.CodyandBob.com

" *Spend less time on things to buy and more time on things to love"*

Dear God,

I'm so grateful for your teaching me that a life helping and inspiring others is a life unmatched in happiness, and fulfillment by anything else. You created everyone for each other, and I thank you for that. Help me to make a positive difference in someone's life each day. Help me to be humble and let someone else make a difference in my life each day too. I humble myself and know that each person you've created is loved and cared for equally by you. Thank you for opening my eyes, heart, and soul to see everyone I share this planet with as my brothers and sisters. I love them. I love me. I love you, dear God. Thank you. Yes... Amen.

♥

GOD MAKES MY LITTLE TAIL WIGGLE
www.CodyandBob.com

" I came here to love "

Dear God,

I am so grateful for my life and the gift of this new day. I came here for a mighty purpose, and one of my life's purposes is to love and help others. Show me how to use every gift, talent, and ability that you've so lovingly blessed me with, to really make a difference in the lives of my brothers and sisters who are your children. I want to help people, inspire them, and make their lives better. Inspire me and show me how to live my life with purpose and passion and to give love and keep giving love as you endlessly fill the love in my heart and soul for myself and to share with every soul I may touch by it. Thank you, God. I love you. Thank you. Yes... Amen.

♥

GOD MAKES MY LITTLE TAIL WIGGLE
www.CodyandBob.com

> ## The right relationships are always easy"

Dear God,

It's so good to know that I don't have to settle for less or second best, or to compromise on what I truly want. I can have any and all of the desires of my heart. I thank you for bringing into my life the best people for the right reasons at just the perfect times for them to be in my life and me to be in theirs. I'm your child. I deserve the most wonderful people and experiences, and I open my belief to allow them in without exception or limitation. The good, the joy, happiness, love, prosperity, abundance, and blessings I can receive are unlimited because you are unlimited. I'm your blessed creation and child. I take all the limits off of you, dear God. I thank you for the truly incredible things you are doing and are about to do in every part of my life. Day by day, in every way, I am getting better and better and more blessed. I love you. Thank you. Yes... Amen.

♥

GOD MAKES MY LITTLE TAIL WIGGLE
www.CodyandBob.com

4

LOVING YOURSELF
AND THE GIFT CALLED
YOUR LIFE

> ## When you look at yourself, you're looking at God"

Dear God,

I am so grateful for this day, this moment, and the gift of life you have given to me. Help me to see myself as you see me, as a child of yours and one who is divinely created and worthy of every blessing and joy from you. Show me that, as I see the divinity that's me, I will also see that same divinity in everyone and everything you have created. Thank you. Yes... Amen.

♥

> ## Many have forgotten that from God they are begotten"

Dear God,

Thank you for this moment to talk to you. In my busy life, I sometimes think about it, yet so often I do not take the time to stop, breathe, think, and be truly grateful for this gift of life you have so lovingly blessed me with. I am so thankful that you created me. I thank you for all the people, animals, and everything in my life—past, present and future—because it all comes from you. Thank you for reminding me each and every day, just how amazing you've created me to be in every way. I love you. Thank you. Yes... Amen.

♥

> ❝
> *Love always finds you
> when you let go"*

Dear God,

You've made everything in this life so simple. Let go of the need for control and let people and things go and let them come back to you in their own divinely perfect way and time. It's taken many years for me to realize this and, now that I do, I cannot even begin to tell you how much happier I feel and my life is. Thank you, God, for showing that to me. Yes, from this day on, I will be the giver of love to any and everyone I meet. And I know what will happen when I do. The more I give love, the more love will be returned to me. Dear God, it's true. I love life and life loves me. Thank you for loving me. I love you, dear God. Thank you. Yes... Amen.

♥

"
Start being good to yourself again and let yourself enjoy the masterfully choreographed play of how your life unfolds each day"

Dear God,

Thank you for showing me how to be my own best friend. Thank you for filling me with your peace, presence, and love and inspiring within me how it feels to be divinely loved by you. I let go of being the critic of my life and anyone else's. I let go of being so demanding, impatient, unkind, and judgmental about anyone and anything. I'm so grateful for your understanding, patience, love, hope, faith, and belief in me, your child, who loves you. You and I are one, dear God. I ask you to guide every area of my life, for I give it all to you. Thank you. Yes... Amen.

♥

5

YOU'VE BEEN CREATED FOR A GREAT PURPOSE

> **You are here because God desires to live and to experience this life, right now, through you, as you"**

Dear God,

I so appreciate you and knowing, truly knowing, that you created me for you so that we could experience all the joys and happiness of my life, in this life, together as one. Thank you so much. I want you to show me how I can let you make my life the most wonderful life it can possibly be. I take the limits off of you, dear God, for all the things you desire to do in my life. I want to touch people's lives in only positive, loving, and empowering ways. Help me to let go of anything and everything that keeps me from experiencing and enjoying the fullness of your blessings. We are one. I love you, dear God. Thank you. Yes... Amen.

♥

GOD MAKES MY LITTLE TAIL WIGGLE
www.CodyandBob.com

> ❝ *If God gave you life, don't you think God can also give you direction?"*

Dear God,

Something very powerful is happening in my life. Now that I look in the mirror, I don't just see the person I am. I see you in me as me. We are one. You are the one who created me. You are the one who keeps me in perfect well being and always will. You are the one who protects me. You are the one who guides me. You are the one who inspires me. You are the one from whom all of my blessings come. And you and I are one, created and living and loving this life for each other. I am so grateful, thankful, and appreciative for anything and everything, dear God. I'm so happy and excited to be living this moment and this day. I cannot wait for tomorrow because we are going to experience brand new things in brand new ways. Thank you for your goodness, your love, and all of your blessings. Thank you for helping me to use every gift, talent, and ability you've so lovingly blessed me with so that we can touch people's lives in such loving, divinely inspired and amazing ways. I love you, God. I am yours, dear God. Thank you. Yes... Amen.

♥

GOD MAKES MY LITTLE TAIL WIGGLE
www.CodyandBob.com

> *You created me to be great, and you gave me the desire to experience it"*

Dear God,

I hear you calling me forward to release the greatness inside of me. Thank you for inspiring me to be bigger, better, happier, and more joyful, and to let myself feel the greatness of who I am and follow your calling wherever you guide me. I let go of the old way of thinking, believing, and experiencing. I am your child; a living, sacred, blessed, and miraculous creation filled with everything you are. Thank you for reminding me that I deserve the greatness you have placed inside of me, along with all the happiness and joys to experience it. I will never stop listening to you, dear God. I love you with all my heart and soul. Thank you. Yes... Amen.

♥

6

THE POWER
OF FAITH TO CHANGE
YOUR LIFE

> **Inside of you is a voice that is always calling you to change"**

Dear God,

I'm so grateful for this day and every day you bless me with. When I was younger, I had so many dreams that made me so happy just thinking about them. As the years have gone by, I know I've let the expectations of life, from others and from myself, push my dreams far back so I won't have to think about them. Yet, all my life, I've known they're still there. They've always been there. They'll always be there because they come from you, dear God. You know better than I or anyone else what it is I love to do, what it is I dream to do, and what it is you know I was created to do. I don't care about my age or anything else. I'm ready to live my dreams. I'm ready for you to take me to every blessing and experience you desire for me. I am here to do your will, dear God. Now I'm ready for you to open all the doors and show me how to do it. I love you, God. Thank you. Yes... Amen.

♥

GOD MAKES MY LITTLE TAIL WIGGLE
www.CodyandBob.com

> ## The four words that can change your life: "Talk to me, God'"

Dear God,

Thank you for this great day. I know you have made me for a purpose greater than that which I've let myself become. I desire to do more, to be more, and to become more. Talk to me, God. Inspire me and show me the right way to go. Thank you for helping me to be who and all you created me to be. Thank you. Yes... Amen.

♥

GOD MAKES MY LITTLE TAIL WIGGLE
www.CodyandBob.com

> " *God doesn't care what you call God... God just wants you to call"*

Dear God,

Your love, power, and presence in my life is unlike anything I'll ever experience from anyone or anything else. I want you to be number one in my life, and I ask that each day you show me how to live my life from your divine blessings and inspiration. I'm so grateful, thankful, and appreciative for it all. You are incredible. I am incredible, and together we are a power unlike anything in this world. Thank you. Yes... Amen.

♥

> *There are unlimited ways to get from where you are to where you next want to go"*

Dear God,

I am so grateful to you for this day and all my blessings. Thank you. What joy it is to know that I don't have to figure it all out to get to where I want and to have what I dream and desire. You are my guide, and I trust you to take me to all the blessings you want me to have and to enjoy. Thank you for being so good to me. Inspire me in ways only you can. Guide me in ways only you know. Help me in ways that come only from you so that I may do your will and follow that will and the life you've created for me wherever you and it take me. Thank you. Yes... Amen.

♥

GOD MAKES MY LITTLE TAIL WIGGLE
www.CodyandBob.com

"We'll lead... you follow"

Dear God,

I'm so thankful that I have you in control of every part of my life. You know every road, every person, every experience I will travel along and have, and the best way to take me from where I am to where I desire to be. I let go of the need to be in control of every detail of my life. You created me. You know me better than I know myself. I gladly give you the reins to my life and ask you to guide, protect, and bless it in your divinely perfect way. Yes God, you lead and I'll happily follow. Thank you. Yes... Amen.

♥

> "There's nothing you cannot have that you have not kept away from yourself. Ask yourself 'Why?' and the answer will change your life."

Dear God,

You know how great I can become. You know what potential and power you've placed inside of me. You know the gifts, talents, and abilities that you've created in me. I thank you so much for showing me and helping me to be everything that you created me to be. I let go of my limited thinking and living any part of my life with limits, doubts, and fears. You are in control of it all. What an awesome feeling it is to know that you, and only you, have my life in your hands and that you're creating me and it to be the amazing masterpiece it will be. I love you, God. Thank you. Yes... Amen.

♥

GOD MAKES MY LITTLE TAIL WIGGLE
www.CodyandBob.com

You give me that stick!"

Dear God,

For so long, I've heard about others' doing extraordinary things and living amazing lives because they have faith and belief. I've always thought I could do that too if I ever wanted to. Yet I've not actually done it the way I know I could. In the way you have been calling me to try. On this day, I'm ready to take a bold leap of faith and belief and begin by giving you some of the control of my life. It's tough for me to say "Here's everything in my life, God; go ahead and take it all and do with it as you please." You know that for me, that is too much too soon, even though I know deep down that's really what I want to do. So I step out in faith, believing and trusting that you know what's best for me, how it's best for me, where it's best for me, when it's best for me, and with those who are best for me. I ask that you take this small part of my life and show me that I can trust you for a little more of it and then a little more of it. Something inside of me is telling me that we're about to have the best time doing this that I can imagine. It's about to get really fun. I'm ready, dear God. I trust you. I believe in you. I have faith in you. I love you. Thank you. Yes... Amen.

♥

GOD MAKES MY LITTLE TAIL WIGGLE
www.CodyandBob.com

> ## "Bark and the door will always be opened"

Dear God,

I am so grateful for the dreams you have placed in my heart. You know the way to them better than anyone. Show me the way to the door that opens to them. Give me the strength and belief to stand patiently and strong until I'm ready and my dreams are ready to become the reality in my life. Thank you. Yes... Amen.

♥

GOD MAKES MY LITTLE TAIL WIGGLE
www.CodyandBob.com

> *God will put you in the perfect place you need to be at the perfect time you need to be there"*

Dear God,

So often—okay, maybe always—I want things to happen when I want them to happen, and it can be frustrating when they don't. Then I realize I can only do so much on my own. Other people have other things important to them and their lives to live and I can't control what they say or do and when they say or do it. It's time for a fresh new way of living my life. One that puts you in the director's chair for the movie called My Life. You, better than I, or anyone else, know where I am, where I've been, and where I'd like to go. You know what will bring me the greatest happiness, joy, fulfillment, and purpose for my life. And you know the best way to take me to them all. I trust in you. I know that everything you do for me—and I'm so grateful for it all—is for my divine perfect, highest, best, and most happy good. Thank you so much for helping and for always being by my side, dear God. I love you. Thank you. Yes... Amen.

♥

GOD MAKES MY LITTLE TAIL WIGGLE
www.CodyandBob.com

> ## *Put yourself into the divine flow and perfect timing for your life"*

Dear God,

Thank you for showing me just how beautifully choreographed this dance of life truly is. Everything just unfolds so perfectly and wonderfully and without my help. Each day, you show me just how in control you are of this world and my life. Thank you for directing it all so amazingly. I so appreciate every moment of every day. I'm so grateful to have the power of my thoughts and to decide how I want to live my life and with whom I want to share it. You are my best friend, my confidant, my protector, and my provider, and I want it to always be that way. Thank you for teaching me that by my choice, whenever I'm in your divine flow, I'll always be guided and know the perfect way for me to go. You are incredible, God. I love you. Thank you. Yes... Amen.

♥

GOD MAKES MY LITTLE TAIL WIGGLE
www.CodyandBob.com

"I'll wait as long as it takes"

Dear God,

Thank you for being so patient, kind, understanding, and loving with me. Thank you for waiting for me to listen to your voice from within and not just listen to it, but have enough faith in myself and in you to follow it. I know now, more than at any time before in my life, you already know what's going to happen in my life for everything, even before anything begins. Today, I know you are so ready to help me, to bless me, and to guide me to every dream in my heart and to all those I've not even let myself go deep inside of me to discover. Take me to it all. I'm ready, dear God. With you, all things are not only possible, they can and will happen in your most divine perfect timing and way that's always for my divine perfect, highest, best, and, yes, happiest good. I love you, God. Thank you. Yes... Amen.

♥

> *I love you for who you are.*
> *Now let me show you who*
> *you can be."*

Dear God,

It amazes me to think how great I can be. There are no limits to what I can have, be, do, or experience. With faith and belief, all things are possible. I'm so grateful and so appreciate your reminding me that I'm your child. I come from you. You are inside of me. You are me and you are for me. And if you are for me, then nothing and no one can be against me. Ever. Thank you, God, for bringing into my life just the best people I so desire who can be good for me and me good for them. I love helping people. I love inspiring people and knowing I'm making a positive difference in their lives. Help me and inspire me to do more, to be greater, and to live an unlimited life of abundance, joy, happiness, love, peace, and fulfillment. It's all because of you, dear God. I love you. Thank you. Yes... Amen.

♥

GOD MAKES MY LITTLE TAIL WIGGLE
www.CodyandBob.com

7

LISTENING
TO THE VOICE
WITHIN

> ❝ *How can you hear the call from within, if so much of your day is spent thinking about the things from without?*"

Dear God,

Thank you for being so good to me. Thank you for reminding me throughout the day that you are my best friend who is always with me, talking to me in ways I can know and understand, guiding me, protecting me, blessing me, and helping me. You know me better than I know myself, and I want to trust you more and more for everything in my life. Thank you for showing me how to do that. Thank you. Yes... Amen.

♥

We're always connected"

Dear God,

I know I live in a bigger world than the one I can see and experience in the here and now. A bigger world where the stars and the universe surround me, and one that you control with absolute perfection. I'm part of that world, for I come from you. I'm your child and your creation, and so are everyone and every animal that has lived and will ever live. I've always wondered what happens to us when we leave these earthly bodies after this life's journey has been completed. I now know my life and who I am will never end. You are eternal, God, and I'm your child that you've created to be eternal just like you. We are one and will always be. The people and animals I love will always be those I love, and they will always love me, because our lives together will never end. We are all eternal and everlasting creations of love and of yours. Thank you for my angels who are always with me, blessing me, guiding me, and helping me. I love you, angels. I love you, God. I love knowing that we are right now and will always be together and forever in each other's lives. I love you, God. I love you, life. Thank you. Yes... Amen.

♥

GOD MAKES MY LITTLE TAIL WIGGLE
www.CodyandBob.com

> *The road you travel is only revealed step by step as you travel it"*

Dear God,

Thank you for helping me to let go of any fear that has kept me from living the life you created me to live. Thank you for showing me that as your divine creation, I have no limits in the life I can live and love except for those I place upon myself by my belief in them. You created me and know everything that brings me happiness. I let go of all limitations and thank you for inspiring me to trust and follow your direction for my life, even when I may not know what the next step may be. You do. I put all my faith and trust in you for my life. I know you are putting everyone and everything in my life in divine perfect order and timing. I love you. Thank you. Yes... Amen.

♥

GOD MAKES MY LITTLE TAIL WIGGLE
www.CodyandBob.com

" *Listen to your angels whispering to you*"

Dear God,

Thank you for all of my angels. So many times in my life, I've felt the hands of a power I never could understand, yet I just knew it was something beyond my control and something unexplainable and unseen. Now I know. It's you and your angels. My angels, who are always with me, guiding me, helping me, blessing me, protecting me, and inspiring me. I'm so grateful to you and to them for it all. Show me how to connect with my angels so that I may do so every day in every way. I love you and all of my friends, family, loved ones, animals, and those I may never have known, yet who know me, who have departed in the physical form from this earth but who are with me right here and right now and will always be. I love you, God. I love you, my angels. Thank you. Yes... Amen.

♥

> ## *Which way are you pointing me to, God?"*

Dear God,

I am so thankful that you are always with me every moment of every day. You are the best friend I could ever ask for. I want to trust my life to your guidance and direction. You, better than anyone else, know what brings me the greatest joy and happiness. You, better than anyone else, know how and why you created me and have given to me the gifts, talents, and abilities you've blessed me with. Thank you for helping me to use them to the fullest of my God-given abilities so that I may touch the lives of your other children and animals in the biggest and best ways. I am so happy and blessed. My life is amazing, and it's all because of you. Thank you. Yes... Amen.

♥

GOD MAKES MY LITTLE TAIL WIGGLE
www.CodyandBob.com

> ## *Let God be good to you"*

Dear God,

I am so grateful for the dreams and desires inside of me. You know exactly what I want and what I need, and the best way to put only those things that are divinely right for me into my life. I give you my life and everything in it, and I thank you for blessing it and guiding it so perfectly in every way. I love you. Thank you. Yes... Amen.

♥

GOD MAKES MY LITTLE TAIL WIGGLE
www.CodyandBob.com

> " *Ask God this: 'How can I let into my life, what you want to put into it?'"*

Dear God,

I'm so ready to let myself start thinking, believing, and expecting a bigger, better life. A life I can live, love, enjoy, and inspire others to. A life where miracle upon miracle of never-ending, never-stopping blessings pour forth from you and rain down and flood my life—a life where I'm using every gift, talent, and ability that you've so lovingly blessed me with to the fullest of my God-given abilities so I can be a blessing to others. I know deep down inside of me that your plans for my life are amazing and are so far above and beyond anything I can know or imagine. From this day on, I let go of any fears, doubts, and worries. By my faith and belief in you, in me, and in us, I release the unlimited power you've placed inside of me to become all that I can be and to live and love the extraordinary life you are calling and taking me to, this day and all the days to come. I love you, God. Thank you. Yes... Amen.

♥

GOD MAKES MY LITTLE TAIL WIGGLE
www.CodyandBob.com

8

FOLLOWING
THE INSPIRATION
WITHIN

> ## When it comes to inspiration... sighs matters"

Dear God,

You more than anyone know what I want and why I want it. I ask that you fill my life with your desires and inspirations because, as my creator, you know exactly the things, experiences, and moments that will bring me the greatest joy, fulfillment, and happiness. Thank you for raining down blessing after never-ending blessing in every part of my life. Let me uplift and be an inspiration to all those I meet. You are such an inspiration to me, dear God, and I love you. Thank you. Yes... Amen.

♥

> ## Ask yourself where you want to go to be the most inspired, and then go there and find out"

Dear God,

Thank you for taking the wheel for the journey called my life. You know just the right ways to go, the perfect timing and ways for us to get there, the right people to meet and places for us to see, and the most fulfilling experiences all along the way. I so appreciate knowing and trusting that my life and everything and everyone in it, is in the best hands with you. You are extraordinary. I am extraordinary. I love you. Thank you. Yes... Amen.

♥

66

This is a great place that's on my way to the next great place"

Dear God,

You have so many great things waiting for me to experience, and on this day I ask you to take me to them. I let go of the attachments I've placed on anything and anyone in my life out of fear. You created me to do more, be more, and have more, and I thank you for every divine desire you have placed inside of me. I'm ready to go anywhere and do anything you want me to. My life is yours, and so is everything in it. Thank you. Yes... Amen.

♥

GOD MAKES MY LITTLE TAIL WIGGLE
www.CodyandBob.com

> *Every moment in every day,*
> *born again in every way"*

Dear God,

I'm so grateful for the blessing and gift of my life, with each new day and with each new moment. A happy life is made up of happy moments, and I ask that you show me to how fill my life with more and more of those happy moments each and every day. For this is the day that you have made, and I want it and will rejoice and be happy in it. Help me to listen to your divine inspiration and guidance. Give me the belief and trust to follow it. I know it is and will always be perfect and just exactly what I want and need at just the perfect time I want and need it. Thank you. Yes... Amen.

♥

GOD MAKES MY LITTLE TAIL WIGGLE
www.CodyandBob.com

"
Where you are is not where you're going to be"

Dear God,

I'm so grateful and thankful for this life you have blessed me with. I'm so thankful for all the things that I've lived so far. Everything and everyone has been a blessing and a teacher on this amazing journey called my life. I'm so excited for all the new that is waiting for me to discover, to live, to love, and to enjoy. I trust you completely to take me to every good thing you have planned for me, and I thank you with all my heart. I love you. Thank you. Yes... Amen.

♥

GOD MAKES MY LITTLE TAIL WIGGLE
www.CodyandBob.com

> **All things work together for everyone's good, at just the right time, and not a moment sooner or later"**

Dear God,

I so appreciate you and the perfect timing for everything in my life. I know at times I can be so impatient because I want things to happen the way I want them to happen and when I want them to happen. Yet, I know deep down, that's not the way life works. It's all in your divine perfect timing for my and everyone else's divine perfect, highest, best good. I trust you for everything in my life. I am so grateful for this day, my life, and all the people and blessings I have in it. I am so happy and excited about all the wonderful blessings and experiences you have planned and are taking me to right now. Thank you. Yes... Amen.

♥

GOD MAKES MY LITTLE TAIL WIGGLE
www.CodyandBob.com

> "When taking action comes from inspiration, it's exhilarating and powerful. When action comes from motivation or guilt, it's rarely satisfying."

Dear God,

Thank you for showing me how to live the inspired life. You created me to have the dreams and desires of my heart, and I'm so grateful that you're showing me how to do so. I sense that my life is changing for the best and the happiest. I let everything you desire to put into my life, come into my life. I can do all things through you. Thank you. I love you. Yes… Amen.

♥

GOD MAKES MY LITTLE TAIL WIGGLE
www.CodyandBob.com

> ## When are you going to let me take you to it?"

Dear God,

Every day and every moment is brand new, and I let go of the old that has helped me get to the bold. I'm at a new place in my life today. I'm a new person and being made fresh and new every minute of every single day. Thank you, God. You are so amazing and wonderful. I open my hands and place them in yours as I hold tightly to you in love, faith, belief, and trust. The rest of my life is going to be the best of my life. I know I have all the time, talent, and ability I'll ever need to do your will and live the life of my dreams. And I know—yes, I truly know deep down inside of me—that you are taking me everywhere you desire and have planned for me to experience and to be. My love for you knows no limits, God. Thank you. Yes... Amen.

♥

GOD MAKES MY LITTLE TAIL WIGGLE
www.CodyandBob.com

9

GOING FROM WHERE YOU ARE TO ANYWHERE YOU WANT TO BE

> *You have the desire because God has the desire to give it to you"*

Dear God,

I thank you for this new day and all the seconds, minutes, and hours in it I will have—to dream big, believe big, expect big, and receive big all the things I so desire. I get the feeling, deep down inside of me, that you can give me anything in this life, if I only I would ask and believe I can have it. I am your child, and I'm worthy of every good and perfect gift that comes from you, dear God. I love knowing that! And even more, I love believing and expecting that! Starting right now, I take the limits off of you and ask that you bring me every joyful and happy desire I have. Take me to every thing and experience you desire for us to have. For your desires are my desires, and my desires are your desires. We are made for each other. We are one for each other. We will always and forever be as one with each other. I love you with everything inside of me, dear God. Thank you. Yes... Amen.

♥

> *If you keep telling the same life story, you'll keep getting the same life experiences"*

Dear God,

You sure know how to get my attention. After years of telling the same old story about my relationships, friends, family, jobs, and experiences, so much of it just makes me unhappy every time I tell it. The message I'm getting from you is, I don't have to tell it or anything to anyone anymore, not even to myself. That I can tell a brand new story, a happier story, an inspiring and uplifting story of the life I'm now living and will be living. Thank you for teaching me that, in my life, what I think about I bring about. With your help, I want to. I will keep my thoughts and words on the things I want, it will bring me happiness when I think about them, and I'm going to let go of the rest. Everything and everyone in my past have all helped me to get to the place I now am, and I'm grateful for them. I bless them and let them go with love and blessings. Today is a new day, one filled with incredible joy and unlimited possibilities for me to be, do, or have anything I can dream and desire. That's the life I choose. That's the life I will live. Thank you, dear God for leading, guiding, and inspiring me to it. I love you. Thank you. Yes... Amen.

♥

> ## *This just in... There's no age limit or expiration date for dreams"*

Dear God,

Thank you for inspiring me with the hope that I can have the dreams I desire, no matter what excuses I've held onto that have kept me from having and living those dreams. I let go of living my life not being authentic to myself or to the things I know deep down I want and will bring me the happiness I seek. You know where I am, and you know the perfect way to get me to where you desire me to be. I put my trust in you and so appreciate every blessing that was, is, and will be to come. Thank you. Yes... Amen.

♥

66

Life will give you whatever you ask"

Dear God,

I can never know how and why so many amazing things in this life happen, yet I know they do. As I look back on my life, there have been many times when the things I hoped for, and even better ones, have happened unexpectedly and it just surprised me. Things I could have never made happen on my own. Things I had no idea were about to happen. Yet you knew. You were the one who made them happen. I've lived my life long enough now to realize there isn't anything called "coincidence" or "chance." Everything in this life and this world happens in divine perfect order, and you are the one orchestrating it all. And you know what's even more amazing? I'm your child. I'm the one you created, and we are forever connected as one. My asking to you is very simple: Guide my life, every part of it, and make it everything you know it can be. It's yours. I'm yours. I am so blessed in every way, and I always will be, every day. And it's all because of you, dear God. I love you. Thank you. Yes… Amen.

♥

GOD MAKES MY LITTLE TAIL WIGGLE
www.CodyandBob.com

> ## God never gives you a dream because it fits your budget"

Dear God,

I'm amazed when I look at the vastness and abundance of everything on this earth and know that you created everything and me. I release my old beliefs in lack and limitation and ask you to replace them with your thoughts of abundance and unlimited possibilities. I'm your child, your creation, and I know deep down inside that what is yours is what can be mine once I believe I can have it and enjoy it. Thank you, God. Yes... Amen.

♥

GOD MAKES MY LITTLE TAIL WIGGLE
www.CodyandBob.com

> *If your dream is important to you, you'll find a way. If it's not, you'll find an excuse."*

Dear God,

I so want to live the life of my dreams. I let go of the fears and excuses. I let go of living my second, third, or anything less than my favorite choices. In their place, I will live my life of doing only the things I dream and desire to do. Yes, dear God, I can have it all because you created me to do anything I dream of, without limits. Thank you for helping and showing me how to do it. While I may not know everything that's going to happen on the way to my dreams, I don't need to know because I trust you to guide me perfectly to every one of them. You've given me the dreams and desires I have for a reason. It isn't my will, dear God, it's your will be done. Your will is my will because it's always for my divine, perfect, and highest, best good, and I love knowing that! Everything you do is because of love. Help me to live my life the same way. Thank you. Yes... Amen.

♥

GOD MAKES MY LITTLE TAIL WIGGLE
www.CodyandBob.com

"Plan your dreams on what you want and not on what you have"

Dear God,

I know I can be either the biggest best friend I'll ever have or the toughest critic I'll ever know. It's all my choice. I want to be good to myself again. I want to be happy, really happy, again. I give you everything in my life and ask that you direct every part of it, so that what I think and what I do is in divine perfect harmony with your incredible and amazing plans for me. I bless all of my thinking and beliefs from the past, every single one of them. Thank you for showing me how they helped me to become who I am and have gotten me to the now where I stand. I'm ready to let those old ideas, attitudes, and beliefs go so that the new, fresh, and inspiring ones can now fill my life and help take me to the greatest life you know is possible and you have planned for me. I can do all things through you, dear God, and I so want to and I will. I love you. Thank you. Yes... Amen.

♥

GOD MAKES MY LITTLE TAIL WIGGLE
www.CodyandBob.com

> *Let everything be a possibility just waiting for you to discover"*

Dear God,

For too long, I've put limits on my life. I've accepted the way others have lived and are living their lives as the way I should do it too. And each time I do so, I feel something deep inside of me saying that's not the way I want to or can live my life. You are calling me forward. You are calling me away from fear, regret, guilt, doubt, and worry. You are calling me to follow you to a greater life, a better life, a happier life, and a life filled with possibilities, just waiting for my dreams. You know how I can live it. Take me to it, God. Let's go there together and live it, love it, and enjoy it. You are inspiring me in ways that are thrilling, exhilarating, and astounding. I hear you talking to me. I hear you telling me, "Expect great things, my child. Expect the very best every day and in every way, and you shall have them." I love you God. Thank you. Yes... Amen.

♥

GOD MAKES MY LITTLE TAIL WIGGLE
www.CodyandBob.com

> **When your head says 'No' and your heart says 'Go,' listen to the one that'll take you to where you're best going to grow"**

Dear God,

The longer I live, the more I realize how blessed and unique I am. There's no one like me and there never will be. I'm me. You created me to be just who I am. My looks, personality, experiences, and the ways I think and dream and desire are all mine and only mine! I love me! I'm so grateful to you for giving me the gift of life. I love it and I love you, God. From this day on, I want to live my life by my dreams. I want to experience everything in this world by my desires. I want the happy kid inside of me to come out and play and be joyful at all the possibilities that can be mine and are waiting for me to discover, have, love, live, and enjoy. I want all of that and every blessing you have planned for me because everything comes from you, dear God. Everything. You are the reason for me, for us, and for it all. My life is yours. I give you my life and everything in it and ask, with love, trust, and all the faith I have, that you guide my life and make it everything I dream of and everything it can be. Thank you, dear God. I love you, dear God. Thank you. Yes... Amen.

♥

GOD MAKES MY LITTLE TAIL WIGGLE
www.CodyandBob.com

> ## *This is only a rest stop on the way to my next stop"*

Dear God,

I am so grateful to you for being so good to me. You have always taken perfect care of me in every way, and you always will. During those times when I become impatient with myself and others, keep reminding me of how far I've come and how much I've grown. Give me your perspective, dear God, that helps me understand and see the bigger picture of my life, that in one year, two years, five years, or however many years from now, so many of the things I'm so focused on right now will be in the rearview mirror and in the past that I've lived, loved, blessed, and let go of. Yes, where I am is not where I'm going or where I'm staying. The new and inspiring are calling me forward and, with you, we're going there together as the best friends who will always be there for each other and loving this life and everything in it with all our heart and soul. I love you so much, God. Thank you. Yes... Amen.

♥

> *Listen to what's calling your name and go answer its call"*

Dear God,

I hear you calling me. I feel it inside of me. It's time for me to be taken to my dreams. I want to live, love, and enjoy every one of them, and I ask for your help to show me how. I give you the "Yes" so that you'll take me to the "grow ahead" I'm being called to. I may not know the way, I may not know the when and where, and that's okay with me. I think about the "Why's" of why I want my dreams, and that's going to take me to all of the "How's" I'll ever need for them to happen. You created me to be great, dear God, and you've given me the desires to live, love, and experience greatness. You are incredible. I am incredible. Together we are an unstoppable force of nature. I love you. Thank you. Yes… Amen.

♥

> ## *It will never stop whispering to you"*

Dear God,

I love knowing that I don't have to know it all or do it all to have the kind of life I dream of. You want to help me. You want to guide me. You want to teach and show me. And you want us to enjoy it all together. From this day on, I will listen to the voice from within, because it is your voice calling me forward to a bigger, better, happier and greater life. Thank you. Yes... Amen.

♥

> ## *Run like you've got the wind at your back"*

Dear God,

You created me for greatness. I feel it. I know it. And I always have. For so long, I've settled for less than I've wanted and that I'm capable of. I've got such power and potential inside of me that's just been waiting to come out and for me to use it. It's not too late to be what I might have been. I'm ready to be that person now. Thank you for whispering to me, by that voice inside of me that is coming from you, that it's not too late, my time to live my dreams hasn't come and gone, and a fresh, new, and exciting next chapter of my life is waiting for me to live it and love it. I'm ready to run like I've got the wind at my back, and with your guidance and inspiration, I'll always know that wind is coming from you. Thank you. Yes... Amen.

♥

GOD MAKES MY LITTLE TAIL WIGGLE
www.CodyandBob.com

10

YOU ARE AMAZING AND YOUR LIFE IS ABOUT TO BECOME EXTRAORDINARY

> **Everybody wants a new beginning. Here's the good news: You can have it anytime you want.**

Dear God,

I love new beginnings. I love knowing my past is not my future and I can begin again every day and in every way. Help me to know what I want and why I really want it. In this world of so much information, so much noise and distraction all trying to get my attention, keep my connection to you open and flowing and always on. Never stop talking to me, guiding me, helping me, taking care of me, inspiring me, blessing me, and loving me. I let go of what was, so you will always have room in my life to bring me what is and what will be. I love you, dear God. Thank you. Yes… Amen.

♥

> *You've come much further than you think"*

Dear God,

So many times I think I'm not getting anywhere and so little in my life ever seems to change. Yet, as I look at where I am now and back at where I've been, it amazes me to realize that so much in my life has changed. I'm not the same person I was ten years ago, and I'll not be the same person ten years from now that I am today. God, I know you've been with me the whole time and you've never left me. You've always been by my side and, whether I realized it at the time or not, you've always been guiding, helping, protecting, and blessing me. I am so grateful and thankful for this and for you. Help me to enjoy this day and all the moments in it, for I am thankful for them all. Help me to start dreaming big things and new ideas again. Show me and inspire me that the rest of my life will be the best of my life. I put everything in it, and everything I am and will ever be, in your hands, dear God. I love you. Thank you. Yes... Amen.

♥

GOD MAKES MY LITTLE TAIL WIGGLE
www.CodyandBob.com

> ❝ *Inside of you right now is the power that will change your life. One day you will decide to use it. How about today?*❞

Dear God,

I've always known there's something inside of me that's bigger than I've ever known. Bigger and greater than I've ever let myself experience. Bigger and far more phenomenal than I've ever let myself become. That power is you, living inside of me. A power so great that it can change my life for the best in the blink of an eye and can help me inspire something in others that can change their lives just as dramatically and wonderfully. Help me to bring it out, dear God. Help me to know it and to use it only for love and blessings and for my own and others' divine best good. Help me to use every bit of it to so I can do your will and keep doing your will for as long as you will bless me with this gift of my life. I'm here to make a difference and to help others. You're my best friend. I love you. Let's change people's lives and our world and do amazing things together. I love you, dear God. Thank you so much. Yes… Amen.

♥

GOD MAKES MY LITTLE TAIL WIGGLE
www.CodyandBob.com

> *Find your rock and stand on it"*

Dear God,

In this life, it's easy to get caught up in the things happening in my life and in others' lives too. Before I realize it, my thoughts and feelings can go off in so many directions. Places where it feels like I'm miles down the road and so far away from the happy place where I was, that at times I can feel a bit lost and unsure of how to quickly get back to where I want to be again. I know I want to be on my rock. To be steady, sure, knowing, secure, and ready to do the things I want to do and follow the dreams I so want to experience. God, I ask that you put me on my rock and keep me on it wherever I go, whatever I think, and whatever I do. I know you are always with me, in me, standing before, behind, and beside me. I know that whenever I feel unsure and my footing and life start to feel a bit shaky, you will always be there holding me, helping me, and never letting me go. You are my best friend, God. I love you. I thank you. Use me to do your will. I'm here for you and for others. You created me to live this life and to love every moment of it. With the gifts, talents, and abilities that you've so lovingly blessed me with, I want us to do amazing things and touch people's lives for the best in any ways we can. I'm ready. I'm unstoppable. I'm yours. Thank you. Yes... Amen.

♥

GOD MAKES MY LITTLE TAIL WIGGLE
www.CodyandBob.com

> *Every street has our name on it"*

Dear God,

With every fiber of my being I know I am great. I know I was born to be great. I know I can be great from this day and this moment on. Thank you for creating inside me the desire to know it, to feel it, to release it, and to be it. As I look around at those in this life who've achieved incredible things and enjoy the things I too desire to have and experience, I ask myself, "If they can have it, why can't I?" After all, they are your children. I am your child. And if some of your children can be mightily blessed, then all of your children can be mightily blessed. From this day and moment on, I want you to be my best friend. I want you to take and guide everything in my life and show me the way, so I can know, be, and do everything you've called and created me to do on this earth. You gave me life for a mighty purpose. You provide for and take perfect care of me because you love me and need me to help you so we can bless others. There is nothing too great for us to do. There is nothing too much for us to have. There is nothing too spectacular that I cannot become. There is no goal or dream too big for us to enjoy. And there is never too much love that I can feel and give to myself and to everyone I meet. We will change the world. And we're going to do it together. You, as my God and creator. And I, as your child who loves you with all of my heart and soul forever. I love you, dear God. I thank you, dear God. Yes... Amen.

♥

GOD MAKES MY LITTLE TAIL WIGGLE

www.CodyandBob.com

Thank you for reading our book!

We'd love to hear your story
at CodyandBob.com,
of how our words and inspirations
have touched your life.

With love and blessings to you,
Bob & Cody

Facebook: /codyandbobinspires
Instagram: @codyandbob

Words That Inspired Me

Words That Inspired Me

Words That Inspired Me

Words That Inspired Me

Words That Inspired Me

Words That Inspired Me

....
....
....
....
....
....
....
....
....
....
....
....
....
....
....
....
....
....
....
....
....
....
....
....
....
....

Words That Inspired Me

Words That Inspired Me

Words That Inspired Me

Words That Inspired Me

....
....
....
....
....
....
....
....
....
....
....
....
....
....
....
....
....
....
....
....
....
....
....
....
....
....
....

Words That Inspired Me

....
....
....
....
....
....
....
....
....
....
....
....
....
....
....
....
....
....
....
....
....
....
....
....
....
....
....

www.ingramcontent.com/pod-product-compliance
Lightning Source LLC
Chambersburg PA
CBHW060313050426
42448CB00009B/1813